Special Days of the Year

Bonfire Night

Katie Dicker

WAYLAND

First published in 2007 by Wayland
Copyright © Wayland 2007

Wayland
338 Euston Road
London NW1 3BH

Wayland Australia
Level 17/207 Kent Street
Sydney NSW 2000

Produced for Wayland by
W White-Thomson Publishing Ltd.
210 High Street,
Lewes BN7 2NH

Editor: Katie Dicker
Designer: Clare Nicholas
Picture research: Amy Sparks
Editorial consultant: Sian Williams

British Library Cataloguing in Publication Data
Dicker, Katie
   Bonfire Night. - (Special Days of the Year)
   1. Guy Fawkes Day - Juvenile literature 2. Gunpowder Plot,
   1605 - Juvenile literature 3. Great Britain - History -
   James I, 1603-1625 - Juvenile literature
   I. Title
   394.2'64

ISBN 978 0 7502 5235 5

Printed in China

Wayland is a division of Hachette Children's Books, an Hachette Livre UK company.

Note: The website addresses (URLs) included in this book were valid at the time of going to press. However, because of the nature of the Internet, it is possible that some addresses may have changed, or sites may have changed or closed down since publication. While the authors and publishers regret any inconvenience this may cause readers, no responsibility for any such changes can be accepted by either the authors or the publisher.

Contents

What are special days?

We use special days to celebrate or remember an important time each year. Special days can be important to a person, a family, a town or even a country.

These boys are celebrating Australia Day on 26 January. This is a reminder of the day in 1788 when the first Europeans moved to live in Australia.

Many countries celebrate a special day in history. One special day in Britain is called Bonfire Night. This has been celebrated for over 400 years. It is a reminder of the day in 1605 when the King of England was nearly killed.

King James I of England ruled from 1603 to 1625.

Robert Winter Christopher wright Iohn wright Thomas Percy Guido Fawkes Robert Catesby Thomas Winter

In 1605, a group of men tried to blow up the Houses of Parliament in London to kill King James I. We call this the Gunpowder Plot. The men knew that on 5 November the King would be in the building with other important people who ruled the country.

These men did not like the way that King James I was running the country. They wanted to kill him.

But their plan did not work. When people found out that the King's life was saved, they lit bonfires to celebrate. Today, we light fires on Bonfire Night, too.

Bonfires are exciting to watch. People gather to feel the heat and to watch the light of the flames.

The story of Bonfire Night

The Houses of Parliament is a government building in London where important laws are made. The men who wanted to kill the King bought a house next to the Houses of Parliament. The house had a **cellar** that went below the government buildings.

The Houses of Parliament is a very famous building in London. This painting (above) shows what the building looked like around the time of the Gunpowder Plot. The building we know today (right) was rebuilt in the 1800s after a fire.

The men stored barrels of **gunpowder** in the cellar. They planned to set them alight to make the building explode. One of the men was called Guy (or Guido) Fawkes. We sometimes call Bonfire Night 'Guy Fawkes Night'.

This actor is pretending to be Guy Fawkes – one of the main people who took part in the Gunpowder Plot.

Why was the King so unpopular?

In 1605, Christians in Britain worshipped in different ways. Some people were **Protestants** and some were **Catholics**. Guy Fawkes and his friends were Catholics.

Protestants and Catholics have different Christian beliefs. Catholic churches (left) have a lot of decoration, but Protestant churches (right) are simpler in style.

At the time, Catholics were treated very badly by the government. They were not allowed to pray and they had to pay money if they did not go to a Protestant church service. Guy Fawkes and his friends thought that, if the King was killed, the laws might change.

Protestants are pulling down statues at this Catholic church. This kind of treatment made the Catholics angry. When King James I ruled, some laws made life very difficult for Catholics.

What happened in 1605?

The King's advisors knew that something was going on. A secret letter had been sent to warn them about the Gunpowder Plot. Soldiers were sent to Parliament to stop the attack. They found Guy Fawkes in the cellar with 36 barrels of gunpowder.

This picture shows soldiers arresting Guy Fawkes. He had gone alone to the cellar to check the gunpowder one last time.

After Guy Fawkes was caught, the King's soldiers punished him. They hurt him to make him tell the soldiers about his friends. The men were all found and later killed for taking part in the Gunpowder Plot.

Guy Fawkes was tortured here, at the Tower of London.

ENTRY TO THE TRAITORS GATE

What happens on Bonfire Night?

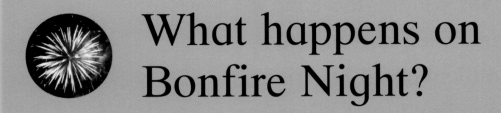

Today on Bonfire Night, people get together in the evening to celebrate. This **tradition** started after Guy Fawkes tried to burn down the Houses of Parliament.

The fires lit on Bonfire Night are made from old pieces of wood that have been collected for many weeks.

'There is a big party in our village on Bonfire Night. The bonfire is really tall and you have to stand back because it is very hot!'

James

16

People also light fireworks made from gunpowder. They are very loud and make the sky look colourful. Other Bonfire Night traditions include eating special food such as cake and toffee.

Sparklers are popular fireworks. If you move them quickly, you can make patterns in the air.

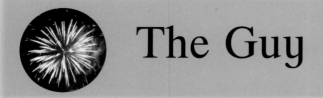

The Guy

People sometimes put a dummy onto the bonfire to remind them of Guy Fawkes. A dummy is a pretend person made from old clothes. It is filled with paper or straw and looks a bit like a scarecrow.

A dummy is put on the fire at many Bonfire Night parties. It is called 'the Guy'. This is short for Guy Fawkes.

Sometimes, children show off the Guy they have made and are given money. There is a lot of competition to make the best Guy!

These boys are asking for 'a penny for the Guy'. They hope to make some money from the Guys they have made.

Fireworks

Fireworks have become very popular on Bonfire Night. Fireworks are made with gunpowder. They were first used in China about 2,000 years ago.

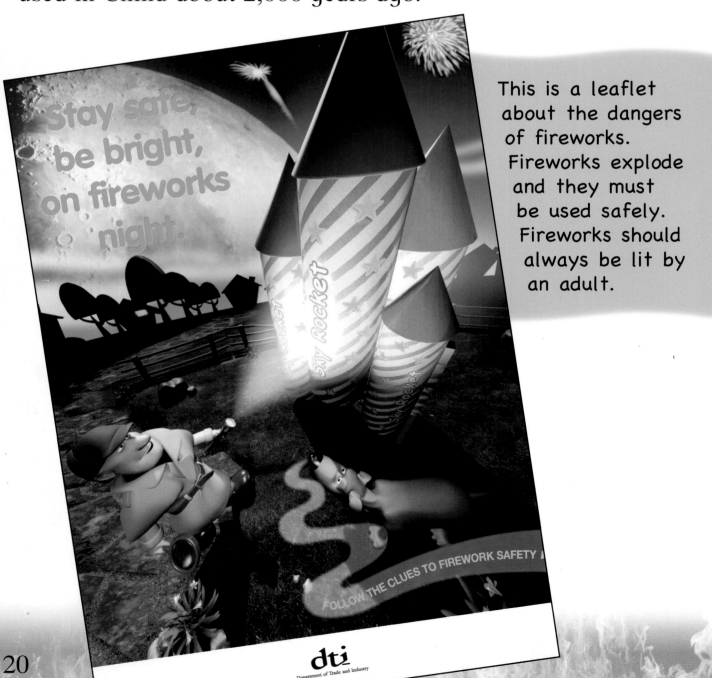

This is a leaflet about the dangers of fireworks. Fireworks explode and they must be used safely. Fireworks should always be lit by an adult.

Stay safe, be bright, on fireworks night.

FOLLOW THE CLUES TO FIREWORK SAFETY

dti
Department of Trade and Industry

Fireworks remind us of the gunpowder that Guy Fawkes tried to use on 5 November. Fireworks are also popular for feasts and celebrations. Some people think that fireworks frighten away evil.

'My favourite fireworks are rockets. It always makes me jump when they go off, and the colours are amazing!'

Joe

Some fireworks explode high up in the sky. They make a loud bang, followed by colourful patterns of light.

In Britain, it is usually cold on Bonfire Night. People like to bake potatoes on the bonfire. They also drink hot soup to keep warm. Other foods include sausages, and sometimes marshmallows for pudding!

Marshmallows taste really good when they are toasted on a fire.

Some people eat a cake called Parkin cake. This is made with lots of treacle and syrup. Apples are sometimes covered in sticky toffee and put onto a stick. We call these 'toffee apples'.

'I help the girls to make toffee apples for their Bonfire Night party. They try to put extra toffee on theirs when I'm not looking!'

Jayne

Toffee apples are easy to make and very tasty.

In Britain, Bonfire Night is celebrated in the autumn. Sometimes, people have a party on the nearest Friday or Saturday to 5 November.

This man is lighting a firework in the garden for his family to enjoy. Other people may choose to go to a big Bonfire Night party.

A town called Lewes in the south of Britain is very famous for its Bonfire Night. People dress up in special costumes. They walk down the street with burning torches. Barrels of tar are also set alight.

These people are walking in the street in Lewes as part of the Bonfire Night celebration.

Bonfire Night around the world

The tradition of Bonfire Night has spread around the world. Many years ago, Britain ruled other countries. The people who lived in these countries started to celebrate Bonfire Night, too.

Today, Bonfire Night parties are still held in Zimbabwe and South Africa.

Bonfires are even lit in countries like New Zealand, which are on the other side of the world. In some countries, Bonfire Night is also known as Fireworks Night, Plot Night or Cracker Night.

Lakes or harbours, such as Wellington Harbour in New Zealand (above), are popular places for big firework displays. This is because the fireworks are reflected in the water.

Glossary and activities

Glossary

Catholics – Christians who follow the teaching of the Roman Catholic church.

Cellar – A room underground.

Gunpowder – A substance that explodes when it is set alight.

Protestants – Christians who do not follow Roman Catholic beliefs.

Torture – Hurting someone to make them tell secrets.

Tradition – Something people have been doing for hundreds of years.

Books to read

- *Guy Fawkes* by Richard Brassey (Orion Children's Books 2005)
- *Bonfire Night* (Don't Forget) by Monica Hughes (Heinemann Library 2003)
- *Guy Fawkes* (Famous People, Famous Lives) by Harriet Castor and Peter Kent (Franklin Watts 2001)

Activities

1. Use other books or ask an adult to help you use the internet to find out more about James I. Why did he not like Catholics?
2. Do you celebrate Bonfire Night? What special things do your family do each year?
3. Make a pretend firework out of old things you've collected.
4. Tell the story of Bonfire Night by making your own cartoon strip.
5. A popular nursery rhyme tells the story about the Gunpowder Plot. Here are the first four lines (below). Using books or the internet, can you find the rest of the verse?

Remember, remember the fifth of November,
Gunpowder, treason and plot.
I see no reason why gunpowder treason
Should ever be forgot.

Useful websites

http://www.guy-fawkes.com
http://www.bonfirenight.net
http://www.fireworksafety.co.uk

Useful address

National Campaign for Firework Safety, Flat 2, 118 Long Acre London, WC2E 9PA

Index